Spotlight on Social Justice

BETWEEN EXTREMES

THE FORMATION AND PRESERVATION OF DEMOCRACY

ELSIE OLSON

TWENTY-FIRST CENTURY BOOKS / MINNEAPOLIS

Twenty-First Century Books™
An imprint of Lerner Publishing Group, Inc.
241 First Avenue North
Minneapolis, MN 55401 USA

For reading levels and more information, look up this title at www.lernerbooks.com.

Main body text set in Bembo Std Regular
Typeface provided by Monotype Typography.

Library of Congress Cataloging-in-Publication Data

Names: Olson, Elsie, 1986–author.
Title: Between extremes : the formation and preservation of democracy / by Elsie Olson.
Description: Minneapolis : Twenty–First Century Books, 2026. | Series: Spotlight on social justice | Includes bibliographical references and index. | Audience: Ages 11–18 | Audience: Grades 7–9 | Summary: "How does political extremism erode democracy? And what are people doing to stop it? Explore the history of democracy, including its origins, the impact of political extremism on it over several decades, how people are working to protect it, and more"—Provided by publisher.
Identifiers: LCCN 2024038753 (print) | LCCN 2024038754 (ebook) | ISBN 9798765644157 (library binding) | ISBN 9798765684955 (paperback) | ISBN 9798765683118 (epub)
Subjects: LCSH: Democracy—Juvenile literature. | Political culture—Juvenile literature. | Political participation—Juvenile literature. | Radicalism—Juvenile literature.
Classification: LCC JC423 .O376 2026 (print) | LCC JC423 (ebook) | DDC 321.8—dc23/eng/20250110

LC record available at https://lccn.loc.gov/2024038753
LC ebook record available at https://lccn.loc.gov/2024038754

Manufactured in the United States of America
1 – CG – 7/15/25

CONTENTS

INTRODUCTION — 4

CHAPTER ONE
DEMOCRACY'S BEGINNINGS — 7

CHAPTER TWO
BUILDING A DEMOCRACY — 13

CHAPTER THREE
A FRACTURED REPUBLIC — 18

CHAPTER FOUR
CHANGING NORTH AMERICA — 23

CHAPTER FIVE
FROM ACTIVISM TO EXTREMISM — 29

CHAPTER SIX
POLARIZATION AND SUPPRESSION — 36

CHAPTER SEVEN
DEMOCRACY IN PERIL — 41

CHAPTER EIGHT
THE FUTURE OF DEMOCRACY — 48

CONCLUSION
BUILDING THE FUTURE — 54

Glossary — 56
Source Notes — 58
Selected Bibliography — 59
Further Information — 60
Index — 62

INTRODUCTION

Every year, hundreds of thousands of voters flock to polling stations around their countries. Each voter declares which leaders they want to represent their interests in their local and national governments. Such elections happen so often that they may appear to be commonplace. Still, each time a person casts a vote, they participate in the ancient system of government known as democracy.

Democracy is a system of government in which laws, policies, leaders, and other government matters are decided directly or indirectly by the people who live under that government. Most historians trace the roots of democracy to ancient Greece. The word *democracy* comes from the Greek word *dēmokratia*. In ancient Greek *demos* means "people." *Kratos* means "rule."

Ancient Roots

The city-state of Athens, Greece, is usually considered the world's first official democracy, dating back more than 2,500 years. But ancient Athenian democracy looked very different from modern democracy. For one, all Athenian citizens were

Athenians would gather at a hill called the Pnyx to vote. Those voting sat facing the speaker's platform (*center*) where new laws were proposed. Athenians would vote by raising their hands.

required to actively participate in their city-state's government. They could vote on any new law that was proposed. Each year, five hundred citizens were selected to govern Athens. If someone didn't fulfill their duties, they were marked with red paint as punishment. However, not all Athenians were considered citizens. Only free, white men could participate in government. This meant people of other genders or races and all enslaved people had no say in the policies and laws that directly impacted their lives.

Athens used a form of government known as direct democracy. This meant that all citizens were directly involved in the city-state's government. This was possible because ancient Athens had a population of about three hundred thousand people. Of those, only about thirty thousand men were considered citizens. Modern democracies often have millions of people. For this reason, nearly all modern democracies, including those in North America, are representative democracies. In a representative democracy, citizens elect government officials to make decisions on their behalf.

Eroding Democracy

Democracy has been established for so long that it can seem sacred and unchangeable. Its principles are deeply embedded in the foundations of countries such as Canada, the US, and Mexico. But democracy as we know it may not be as secure or permanent as it seems. Just a few hundred years ago, women, Black people, and Indigenous people in North America had no say in the laws or leaders that governed them. Voter suppression, political polarization, and social inequality have continued to threaten hard-won rights and liberties.

When democracy erodes, the principles of fairness, equality, and representation weaken. Political extremism erodes democracy by promoting rigid, uncompromising views that can lead to division and conflict. Political extremists use violence and misinformation to spread distrust and fear in the name of radical beliefs. This can make people lose trust in institutions including the government, courts, and media. People may start believing that these institutions do not represent them and that their voices are not heard. This distrust can lead to a breakdown in the cooperation necessary for democracy to function well.

Still, there is hope for democracy. Activists are working to fight voter suppression and engage more people in the electoral process. Elected leaders are working to pass laws that protect voter rights and limit online extremism. And voters turn out each Election Day to ensure their votes are counted and their voices are heard.

CHAPTER ONE

Democracy's Beginnings

Many regard Athens as the first fully functioning Western democracy. But the roots of democratic government go much further back than ancient Greece. Ancient tribes of hunter-gatherers likely made group decisions using a form of democracy. About 4,500 years ago, the first public assemblies appeared in parts of the Middle East that now make up Syria, Iran, and Iraq. During these assemblies, citizens debated and discussed laws and ideas and made decisions as a group. Similar assemblies called sanghas soon spread to Buddhist monasteries in what is now India. Sanghas were assemblies in which the members of a monastery made decisions together.

North American Democracy

Democratic ideas also sprang up in parts of North America, independent of Greek influence. Around the fourteenth century, a group of five Indigenous nations, the Mohawk, Oneida, Onondaga, Cayuga, and Seneca, joined together to form a complex political system known as the Iroquois Confederacy. A council of leaders, in which each nation was

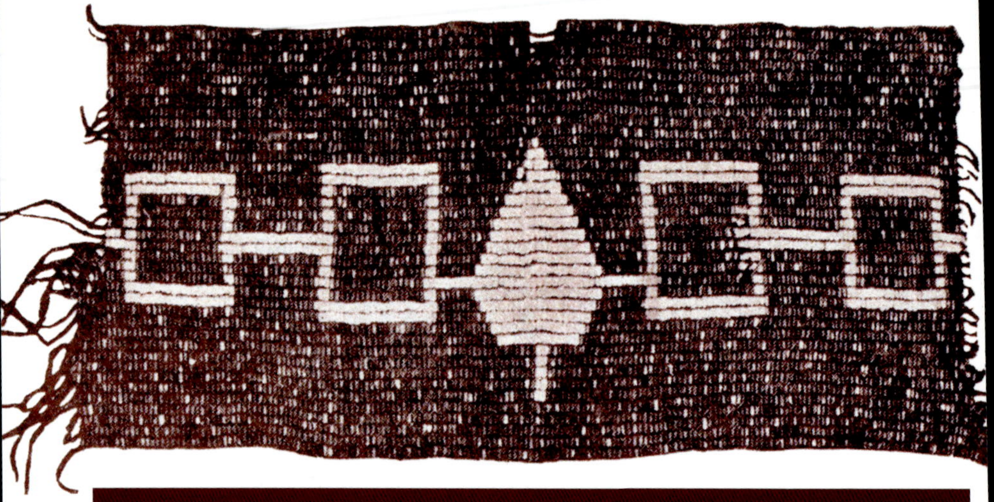

The Hiawatha belt symbolized peace among the nations of the Iroquois Confederacy. Each connecting symbol represented one nation. The belt's design was so important that it became the flag of the Iroquois Confederacy.

represented, made decisions. The oldest woman in each clan, known as the clan mother, chose the chiefs. All confederacy decisions had to be unanimous. The Iroquois Confederacy is the oldest continuous representative democracy. It helped lay the foundation for federal governments including those of the US and Canada.

Archaeologists have also found evidence of ancient democracies in what is now Mexico. A senate of one hundred men governed the city of Tlaxcallan and made decisions on behalf of the citizens. Becoming a Tlaxcallan senator was not an easy task. Candidates had to survive two years of intense training, during which they were schooled in the city's laws.

Across the Atlantic

Across the Atlantic Ocean, Greek and later Roman democracies rose and fell. By 500 CE, scattered feudal kingdoms comprised most of Europe. Feudalism is a form of government in which a kingdom's land is dispersed among nobles who agree to provide military service to a monarch. Peasants known as serfs farm the land in exchange for protection from the nobility. Each feudal kingdom functioned as an autocracy governed by a single leader with nearly full decision-making control. Such leaders were often kings or queens who were born into the role rather than elected. Many monarchs were more concerned with themselves than with the well-being of their people. In the 1500s, King Henry VIII of England executed more than fifty thousand people. He nearly caused his country to go bankrupt thanks to his lavish lifestyle.

However, not all monarchs were unfit for the job. Some were benevolent leaders committed to serving their people. Such monarchs were often trained for the role from birth. They surrounded themselves with talented advisors and tried to do what was best for the people they ruled. One of the best-known benevolent leaders was Indian emperor Ashoka. In the 200s BCE, he adopted a policy of nonviolence and encouraged his people to live freely according to their beliefs. Ashoka founded hospitals, built roads, and passed laws banning animal cruelty.

The Enlightenment

Under feudalism, religion was closely intertwined with government. Monarchs ruled under a principle known as the divine right of kings, which stated that their power came directly from God. This made their power absolute and not subject to any other person. However, other institutions could influence monarchs. During the Middle Ages (500–1500), the Catholic Church was extremely wealthy and powerful.

It influenced monarchs and suppressed other religious beliefs, often through violence.

During the Age of Enlightenment (1685–1815) a group of thinkers questioned the role of religion in government. They advocated for reason over faith. English philosopher John Locke questioned the divine right of kings and argued for religious tolerance. In the 1640s English Parliament rebelled against the king during a series of civil wars. The first English political parties emerged in the years that followed. In the 1700s Swiss philosopher Jean-Jacques Rousseau preached democratic principles, including basic human rights. He argued for equality and liberty for all people and that a government's laws should support the common good, making life better for its citizens.

John Locke believed in the separation of church and state. He argued that government should focus on protecting individual rights and maintaining social order while religious matters should be left to individual beliefs. Locke's ideas on limited government and individual freedom played a crucial role in shaping the US Constitution.

The Magna Carta was originally written in Latin and contains sixty-three clauses. Many of these clauses included legal rights, such as an individual's right to inherit property, and protection from unlawful imprisonment. In later centuries, people cited the Magna Carta as a guarantee of basic human rights.

The Magna Carta

On June 15, 1215, King John of England signed a document that challenged his divine right to rule. This was the first written document stating a king was not above the law. After several wars, King John tried to rebuild his country's treasury by demanding payments from English nobles. This made him unpopular with his people. In 1215 a group of nobles declared civil war on the king. Eventually, the nobles agreed to end the war if the king signed a document called the Magna Carta. The document laid out a series of basic rights that limited the king's power. These included the right to a trial, property protections, and the right for the nobles to declare war on the king if he refused to honor the document. The Magna Carta primarily addressed the concerns of the wealthy and powerful nobles. Low-income people were not involved in its creation. Still, it was the earliest version of England's constitution. The Magna Carta laid the foundation for constitutions around the world, including those of the US and Canada.

Spreading Out

As the Age of Enlightenment began, European nations explored and colonized new places. England, Spain, and France had all established colonies in North America and were fighting for control of the continent by the 1600s. The European colonists brought their ideas about government and religion to North America. They forced these ideas and beliefs on the millions of people already living on the continent. By the mid-1700s millions of European colonists had settled in what is now Canada, the US, and Mexico. But kings and queens thousands of miles away still governed them. Some colonists began to feel that these monarchs did not have their best interests at heart.

King George III reigned over Great Britain and Ireland from 1760 to 1820. His policies asserted more control over the American colonies. The Stamp Act of 1765 required colonists to pay a tax on every piece of printed paper they used, such as newspapers and legal documents. The Townshend Acts of 1767 added taxes on more items and the money was used to pay British officials in the colonies. These actions were seen as oppressive by the colonists and fueled their desire for independence.

CHAPTER TWO

Building a Democracy

On December 16, 1773, thousands of American colonists gathered in Boston Harbor under the cover of darkness. A group of men disguised as Indigenous Americans climbed aboard a cargo ship loaded with tea. One by one, the men threw 342 chests of British tea overboard. This was an act of protest against a recent series of taxes the British king had passed on the colonies. Many colonists felt these taxes were unfair because the American colonies had no representation in British Parliament. Britain's King George III appointed colonial governors. The colonists had little say in the laws that governed them. The Boston Tea Party, as the event became known, was a way to make their voices heard. But according to the colonial governor of Massachusetts, the event was a high-handed riot.

Protest or Extremism?

The Boston Tea Party was a peaceful act of protest. No one fired any shots, and no one was injured. The protesters even tidied up the ship afterward. But not all colonial protests were as peaceful. Some even tilted toward extremism. Earlier protests had resulted in anti-British colonists, known as Patriots, physically attacking British soldiers and destroying the homes of British officials. Still, Patriot leaders urged protesters to remain peaceful. "No mobs, no confusion, no tumult," became a slogan for the movement.

The American Revolution began on April 19, 1775, with a minor battle in Massachusetts. Great Britain and its American colonies fought over colonial independence for eight years. Finally, on September 3, 1783, British forces surrendered. The United States was a free and independent nation. The hard work of building a government began.

Designing a Democratic Republic

In May 1787 a group of Patriot leaders, who became known as the founding fathers, gathered in Philadelphia, Pennsylvania, to design a government. After three months, they emerged with the US Constitution. This is the document that still serves as the foundation for US law. The document was the result of debate and compromise. Many founders feared giving the government too much power. They worried about creating the same kind of authoritarian government they had just rebelled against. Other founders worried that not giving the government enough power would make it too weak to be effective.

In the end, the founders decided on a democratic republic. In a republic, voters elect leaders to represent them. In a pure democracy, voters are directly involved in lawmaking and governing. In the US, elected leaders representing the people would govern the nation. The government was divided into three branches: legislative, judicial, and executive, each with unique and limited powers and responsibilities. The founders felt this organization would allow each branch to oversee the others and prevent any branch from gaining too much power.

Thirty-nine out of fifty-five delegates signed the US Constitution on September 17, 1787. Some delegates decided against signing it because the document did not include a bill of rights. Others chose not to sign the Constitution because it protected enslavement.

Left Out

The US Constitution established a government by the people and for the people. But in the 1780s the idea of what *people* meant was very different than it is today. The founding fathers were exclusively landowning white men, and only white, landowning men were eligible to vote. Some states even barred non-Christians from voting. Millions of women, Black people, and Indigenous people had no voice in their country's government.

REFLECT

How did the exclusion of women, Black, and Indigenous people influence the laws and structure of the young US government?

Writer Mercy Otis Warren criticized the Constitution as doing too little to protect regular people's rights, writing:

> . . . a Constitution, which, by the undefined meaning of some parts, and the ambiguities of expression in others, is dangerously adapted to the purposes of an immediate aristocratic tyranny . . .

Political Parties Emerge

In the spring of 1789, the first inaugurated US president George Washington and the first US Congress gathered in New York to begin operating under the newly ratified Constitution and establish the federal government. But almost immediately, divisions that had begun during the crafting of the Constitution turned into fractures between groups of founders. These fractures became the foundation of the first US political parties.

The first US Congress was known as the First Federal Congress. It lasted from 1789 to 1791 and laid the foundation for future US Congresses.

On one side, the Federalists, which Secretary of the Treasury Alexander Hamilton led, favored a strong central government. Thomas Jefferson led the Anti-Federalists, later known as the Democratic-Republicans. This party argued for a weaker central government and stronger states' rights. The parties largely split along geographical lines, with Federalists representing the northeast and mid-Atlantic states and the Democratic-Republicans having ties to the southern states.

The French Revolution

People often describe political parties around the world using the terms *left-wing* and *right-wing* or *left* and *right*. These terms originated from the French Revolution. In July 1789 a group of French revolutionaries stormed the Bastille. This was a massive Parisian fortress used as a prison. The revolutionaries released political prisoners and demanded the king step down. The rebels formed a national assembly to act as the revolution's new government. Factions in the assembly disagreed about the extent of power the French king should retain. Those sitting on the *right* of the assembly president argued that the king should retain veto power, a more traditional view. Those sitting on the president's *left* believed the king should retain no veto power. This was more radical. After years of fighting, the left prevailed, and the king was put on trial and later executed in 1793. France became a republic in 1792, but it was short-lived. French emperor Napoleon Bonaparte overthrew the revolutionary government and reestablished France as an autocracy in 1804.

The revolutionaries who stormed the Bastille were mostly store owners and craftspeople who lived in Paris. The event was important because it symbolized the end of the old order and paved the way for the radical transformation of French society.

CHAPTER THREE

A Fractured Republic

In the early years of the US government, a key issue divided the new nation—enslavement. While enslavement had been legal throughout the British colonies, most of the five hundred thousand enslaved people lived in the South. Starting in 1780 northern states began to outlaw enslavement. Meanwhile, southern states relied on enslaved laborers to grow profitable crops, such as cotton and tobacco. Many northerners began to disagree more with enslavement while southern leaders sought to expand the practice. As territories became US states, leaders argued over whether to allow enslavement in the new states. By 1820 the United States was home to more than 1.5 million enslaved Black people. Half of the states were free, meaning enslavement was against the law. The other half allowed enslavement.

Around this time, new political parties were emerging. By the 1820s the Federalists had fallen out of power. The Democratic-Republicans were divided over whether to support Andrew Jackson for president. The election of 1828 was much less civil than previous elections, with both sides using the media to launch personal attacks on the presidential candidates and their families. In the end, Jackson won the election, and the Democratic-Republicans split into the pro-Jackson Democratic Party and an anti-Jackson party known as the Whigs. The Democrats largely represented farmers from southern states and supported a less powerful federal government and more individual freedoms. Whigs favored stronger government and supported more humanitarian issues, including public schools and prison reform.

At Jackson's inauguration in 1929, crowds of supporters flooded the White House, celebrating wildly and damaging furniture in their excitement. This was the first time an inauguration turned into a large public gathering.

A Nation Divided

By the 1840s the Whig Party was at war with itself over the issue of enslavement. In 1849 California was ready to join the US as a free state. This would mean free states outnumbered enslavement states, giving them greater legislative power. Southern states threatened to secede from the US over the issue. In the end, a compromise emerged. But the compromise permanently fractured the Whig Party. Northern Whigs formed the anti-enslavement Republican Party, while Southern Whigs joined with the pro-enslavement Southern Democrats.

The national divisions over enslavement soon turned from tension to terror. Extremist groups on both sides practiced intimidation and violence. Armed abolitionists flooded Kansas Territory, hoping to influence the territory's decision about whether to outlaw enslavement. Meanwhile, pro-enslavement forces stormed the anti-enslavement town of Lawrence, Kansas,

Nat Turner's Rebellion

In August 1831 Nat Turner led the first and only successful US rebellion by enslaved people. Turner was born into enslavement in Virginia. On August 21 Turner and a group of seven other enslaved men murdered the family that enslaved them. They traveled to the nearby town of Jerusalem, Virginia, killing any white person they encountered and rallying other enslaved men to their cause. Turner and his followers killed more than sixty people over the next few days before the local militia confronted them. Turner hid for six weeks before being captured and hanged. Turner's extreme tactics divided Americans. Abolitionists and many enslaved Black people felt Turner's actions were justified and praised him as a hero. White Southerners were frightened and horrified. The rebellion led to more extreme restrictions on enslaved people throughout the South.

destroying buildings. The violence lasted for several years, until Kansas was officially admitted as a free state in 1861. The same year, Republican Abraham Lincoln was inaugurated as president. By April, many Southern states had seceded from the Union. The Civil War (1861–1865) had begun.

Free at Last?

The Civil War ended with a Northern victory in April 1865. The war had devastated the South. But it had ended enslavement. Black people across the US were officially free. But they soon found that free did not necessarily mean equal.

In the 1800s racial prejudice was commonplace across the US. Even many abolitionists didn't believe that Black people deserved equal treatment, rights, or respect. This racism did not end with the Civil War, and as a result many Black people struggled to find their place in US society and its governance. In July 1868 the Fourteenth Amendment granted citizenship to "all persons born or naturalized in the US." This included Black people, which theoretically gave Black men the right to vote. Black voters went to the polls, mainly supporting the Republican candidates who had fought to end enslavement.

Many Southern white Democrats resorted to extreme tactics to suppress Black voters. They formed secret terrorist groups, including the Ku Klux Klan and Knights of the White Camellia. Terrorist organizations use fear, intimidation, and violence to advance their political beliefs. These groups aimed to suppress Black liberties, including the right to vote. In September 1868, just a few months after the Fourteenth Amendment passed, the Knights of the White Camellia massacred more than two hundred people in Opelousas, Louisiana. Most of those killed were Black men and women. The violence was meant to discourage Black people from voting in the upcoming presidential election.

On February 25, 1870, Hiram Revels became the first Black lawmaker in the US when he was elected senator for the state of Mississippi.

In 1870 Congress passed the Fifteenth Amendment to the Constitution, which guaranteed Black men the right to vote. Federal troops helped support this law, protecting Black voters as they went to the polls. In many Southern states, Black people nearly outnumbered white people in population. This gave them power at the polls. By 1877 more than two thousand Black people held public office in the US.

"The right of citizens of the United States to vote shall not be denied or abridged by the United States or by any state on account of race, color, or previous condition of servitude."

—The Fifteenth Amendment

Suppressing the Vote

In 1877 President Rutherford B. Hayes removed the federal troops protecting Black voters. Southern Democrats soon found new ways of discouraging Black voters through racist policies and further violence. Poll taxes required prospective voters to pay an expensive fee to cast a ballot. Literacy tests required voters to pass a challenging, sometimes impossible, written test. Grandfather clauses only allowed a person to vote if their grandfather had also voted, leaving out most Black southerners, who were descended from enslaved people. Such laws disproportionately affected Black voters, who often had little to no money or formal education. To make matters worse, many election officials chose not to require white voters to meet the policies. Political parties would repeatedly use such tactics over the next one hundred years to achieve their desired results at the polls.

REFLECT

What are some long-term implications that might come from suppressing Black voters in the 1800s? How might these implications affect modern US citizens?

CHAPTER FOUR

Changing North America

By the turn of the twentieth century, North America was changing, and democracy was spreading, including in Mexico. The country had won its independence from Spain in 1821. In 1824 it established itself as a democratic republic inspired by its northern neighbor, the US. Mexico's federal government divided the country into nineteen states. However, for the next sixty years, the nation remained divided into conservative and liberal groups that fought for government control.

Democracy in Name Only

In 1877 liberal dictator Porfirio Díaz took control of Mexico. Under Díaz, low-income people had few rights. Wealthy plantation owners stole and used their land. Those who protested were arrested or murdered. While elections were held during Díaz's reign, they were not free or fair.

By 1910 many Mexicans had had enough. They rebelled against Díaz's leadership, fighting for the democracy they had been promised. Rebels overthrew Díaz and elected a new leader, Francisco I. Madero. However, another rebel leader overthrew Madero in 1915. The chaos continued, and several additional leaders took control before Alvaro Obregon became president in 1920. Obregon and subsequent presidents granted more rights to low-income and working-class Mexicans, including the right to form unions. But throughout this period, Mexico remained a primarily authoritarian government.

The Rise of the Far Right

Across the ocean in Germany, a new conservative party was rising to power. The far-right Nazi Party formed in 1919. It strongly opposed democracy and sought to purge the country and later the world of any non-white or non-Christian person as well as anyone who disagreed with the party's ideas. In 1933 Nazi leader Adolf Hitler became Germany's chancellor, and the country became a dictatorship. The government limited its citizens' rights and liberties and began a genocide principally targeting Jewish people, but also LGBTQ+ people, Black people, political opponents, and those with physical or mental disabilities. Germany soon began invading nearby countries, leading to World War II (1939–1945). Eventually, Germany was defeated, but the far-right beliefs never entirely faded away. Former Nazis hid in the US and Canada to avoid being punished for their war crimes. Neo-Nazi groups, or modern groups supporting Nazi ideology, would rise around the world and have continued to sow chaos. These groups hold strong white supremacist beliefs. They are known to commit hate crimes from beatings to murder.

Independent Canada

In 1931 Canada became independent from Great Britain. However, Canada had been functioning as a democracy before then. In 1867 Canada was divided into several provinces and established a parliament. In the same year, Canadians developed their constitution based on the British Constitution. The Canadian Constitution allowed Canadians to elect their leaders and largely govern themselves, but British leaders had to approve any changes.

Canada continued to expand its territory and gradually gained more independence from Great Britain. In 1918 Canada passed a law granting new liberties to half its citizens when it gave women the right to vote. However, this law didn't apply equally to all Canadian women. It still barred Indigenous and Asian women from voting.

Voting Rights and Restrictions

Before Canada made it legal, women's voting rights had already been spreading like wildfire around the world. New Zealand became the first country to grant women the right to vote in 1893. By 1900 a handful of western US states allowed women to vote, but activists wanted more. They had held meetings and gave speeches since the 1840s, advocating for a federal law granting women voting rights. By the early 1900s the movement had gained steam. In 1916 Jeannette Rankin of Montana became the first woman elected to the US House of Representatives. More

REFLECT

Why do you think it took so long for women to gain the right to vote in Canada and the US? What challenges do you think different groups of women faced in voting after its legalization?

and more politicians, including Democratic president Woodrow Wilson, publicly supported suffrage.

In 1920 Congress passed the Nineteenth Amendment, granting women in the US the right to vote. However, the law didn't mean all women could go to the polls. The same racist laws and policies that prevented Black men from voting also disenfranchised Black women. Indigenous people were still not considered US citizens, barring them from casting their ballots. In 1924 the federal government passed the Snyder Act, officially making Indigenous people US citizens and granting them voting rights.

Other changes were in store for US democracy. Much of the world, including the US, suffered an economic recession, the Great Depression (1929–1941). Different political parties proposed various solutions to help people during this time. The political parties that had been in place for decades underwent large ideological changes. Democrats

"A man's rights rest in three boxes. The ballot box, jury box and the cartridge box. Let no man be kept from the ballot box because of his color. Let no woman be kept from the ballot box because of her sex."

—Abolition leader Frederick Douglass

Rankin won a seat in the House of Representatives for a second time in 1940. During her time in Congress, she voted against getting involved in both world wars. Because of her passion for peace, she was nicknamed the Original Dove in Congress.

Bloody Sunday

On March 25, 1965, Martin Luther King Jr. (*front center*) led nonviolent demonstrators into Alabama. The violence on Bloody Sunday had shocked the public, strengthened support for the civil rights movement, and ensured the march to Montgomery was under federal protection.

In 1963 less than 2 percent of eligible Black voters were registered to vote in Selma, Alabama. This low registration rate was due to racist policies designed to make it difficult for Black people to register. The voter registration office was only open two days a month, and Black applicants had to complete long, complicated forms and pass difficult tests.

Protests against these discriminatory policies had previously resulted in violence against the peaceful demonstrators, including the death of a young Black man, Jimmie Lee Jackson. On Sunday, March 7, 1965, more than six hundred civil rights protesters began to march out of Selma, Alabama, in protest of these injustices and the violence they faced. They planned to march to the state capital, Montgomery. The protesters had marched only a few blocks when law enforcement stopped them. The officers attacked the protesters, tear-gassing them, beating them with clubs, and hurling insults. Throughout the attack, the protesters remained peaceful. More than fifty of the activists were hospitalized for their injuries. The event became known as Bloody Sunday. The treatment the marchers faced horrified many people across the US. Other marches sprang up across the country as thousands of activists joined the cause. A week later, US president Lyndon B. Johnson presented the Voting Rights Act to Congress.

now favored a strong federal government, more social programs, and liberal policies. Republicans now supported conservative policies, including a weaker federal government.

The Civil Rights Movement

More changes awaited a huge group of US voters. Black southerners were fed up with racist laws affecting their civil liberties, including voting rights. They held massive protests in the 1950s to demand an end to this unequal treatment. At the time, much of the South was segregated. Civil rights activists demanded the right to attend the same schools, ride the same buses, and use the same public spaces as white people. They also called for an end to policies such as poll taxes that limited their right to vote.

Extremist white supremacist groups, such as the Ku Klux Klan, targeted civil rights leaders and their families, burning homes and churches and murdering people. Although activists often faced such violence, the civil rights movement of the 1950s and 1960s relied almost exclusively on peaceful tactics, such as boycotts and sit-ins.

"Do you know I've never voted in my life, never been able to exercise my right as a citizen because of the poll tax? . . . I can't pay a poll tax, can't have a voice in my own government."

—Black Georgia voter George Trout, 1930s

In 1965 Congress passed the Voting Rights Act. This law barred discriminatory voting practices such as poll taxes. It guaranteed all US citizens the right to vote, regardless of their race. The act was a huge victory for the civil rights movement. But in the coming years, new laws and policies would erode the rights activists fought so hard to gain.

CHAPTER FIVE
From Activism to Extremism

As civil rights supporters protested across the US, many young people were rallying for a different cause. In the wake of World War II, Asian and European leaders divided Vietnam into two nations. North Vietnam had a Communist government while South Vietnam functioned as a democracy. However, North Vietnam leader Ho Chi Minh wanted to reunite Vietnam under his rule.

Since the 1950s the spread of Communism had terrified Americans. The US's main political rivals were Russia and China, both Communist nations. US leaders feared that if Vietnam reunited as a Communist country, Communism would spread across Asia. In 1965 the US joined the Vietnam War (1955–1975), fighting for South Vietnam. By 1969 the US Army drafted almost two million Americans to join the fight. But many Americans, especially young people, strongly opposed their country's involvement in the war. They didn't want to be forced to fight in a war they didn't believe in.

Anti–Vietnam War activists held protests at college campuses across the nation. The national student organization Students for a Democratic Society (SDS) organized the first protests. But the movement spread throughout the 1960s as

In May 1970 approximately four million young people participated in anti–Vietnam War protests that shut down classes at more than seven hundred colleges, universities, and high schools in the US. Many schools remained closed for the rest of the spring semester.

more young people were drafted into military service. Although the protests were mostly peaceful, many ended violently when law enforcement clashed with activists. In 1970 a protest at Kent State University in Ohio ended with officers shooting thirteen students, four of whom died. Later that year, more than twenty thousand protesters held a march in Los Angeles. Known as the Chicano Moratorium, the marchers protested the disproportionate number of Latine soldiers killed in the war. (*Chicano* is a term Mexican Americans created and use to describe people of Mexican American culture and heritage.) Police confronted the peaceful protesters, leading to three deaths, two hundred arrests, and hundreds

Extremism or Activism?

Extremism and activism can be tricky to tell apart. Activism is the practice of using direct and forceful actions to support or oppose an often-controversial issue. Some experts define extremists as activists who commit acts of violence to harm others or who show disregard for human lives and safety. Under this definition, activists who perform illegal acts such as certain kinds of protesting, vandalism, and property destruction are not extremists, as long as the activists take steps to ensure no people are harmed. Many nonviolent protests, such as the Chicano Moratorium or the Kent State protest, become violent when authorities clash with protesters. However, the activists, not the authorities, are usually the ones harmed. In other situations, individual activists instigate violence during otherwise peaceful demonstrations. These activists may even be from opposing groups, hoping to paint the protests negatively. In 2020 a man linked to a white supremacist group was seen smashing windows during Black Lives Matter protests in Minneapolis, Minnesota. This was the first act of destruction in a previously peaceful protest. But the act caused the protest to escalate into further property destruction.

The Black Lives Matter protests in 2020 began after a police officer killed George Floyd. His death sparked widespread demonstrations across the US and Canada. These protests called attention to police brutality and injustices faced by Black Americans.

of injuries. Similar protests spread across the nation. The US government soon recognized how unpopular the war had become. The US began pulling troops out of Vietnam, and by 1975 the war was over.

Left-Wing Violence

While the SDS and other liberal protest groups largely used nonviolent tactics, some extremist offshoots of these groups took violent measures. In the late 1960s a branch of SDS called Weather Underground formed to advance Communism and fight for social issues through violent revolution. By 1976 the group had claimed responsibility for twenty-five bombings of federal buildings. They were also charged with robberies and murders.

In 1974 a left-wing Socialist extremist group, the Symbionese Liberation Army (SLA) made headlines when they kidnapped wealthy college student Patty Hearst. After months in captivity, Hearst appeared to adopt the SLA's beliefs and joined her captors' illegal practices. The SLA committed multiple robberies, murders, and bombings aimed at countering racism, capitalism, and Fascism before a clash with law enforcement led to the arrests of some and deaths of others in 1975.

Ecoterrorism

Other left-wing activist groups focused on protecting the environment. Throughout the 1970s and 1980s, Americans became increasingly concerned about how human activity was affecting the planet. The government passed new laws to protect animals and limit pollution, but many environmentalists believed more action was necessary. Some

After Hearst was kidnapped, SLA members forced her to speak out against her wealthy parents and participate in two robberies. She was arrested and convicted of bank robbery in 1975. She spent twenty-two months in jail.

environmentalists took radical actions, which became known as ecoterrorism.

Most environmental groups focused on nonviolent acts, such as staging sit-ins in trees to prevent logging or damaging property and sabotaging equipment. Animal rights groups released captive animals intended for use in research. But in 2009 animal rights activist Daniel Andreas San Diego became the first-ever domestic terrorist to be placed on the Federal Bureau of Investigation's Most Wanted list after bombing a biotechnology company. He was never captured. San Diego was a member of a group called Stop Huntingdon Animal

Cruelty. The group targeted companies that worked with Huntingdon Life Sciences, a company that frequently used animal testing and experimentation in its research. Animal rights terrorism peaked in the late 1990s and declined in the years following San Diego's attack. Many activists accused law enforcement of unjustly targeting animal rights groups, since no animal rights related attack had ever caused a human death.

REFLECT

Based on the definition of extremism in this chapter, do you think ecoterrorism is extremism? Why or why not

Religious Extremism

Throughout the 1980s and 1990s many extremist activities were tied to specific social issues, such as environmentalism or reproductive rights. But broader extremist groups also formed. Many of these were tied to specific religious beliefs. The mid-1980s saw the rise of the Christian Identity Movement (CID). Groups associated with CID used the Christian Bible to justify acts of white supremacy and antisemitism. Members engaged in acts of violence and terrorism, from murdering prominent Jewish disc jockey Alan Berg to mass shootings in Jewish synagogues. One of the best-known CID groups was the Aryan Nations. The Aryan Nations was closely associated with the rise in neo-Nazism, which gained popularity in the US and Canada throughout the 1990s. By 1996 the Aryan Nations had chapters in twenty-seven states.

Religious extremism was not just an issue in North America. Extremist groups were on the rise around the world. On September 11, 2001, terrorists tied to Al Qaeda, an Islamic extremist group, crashed hijacked planes into buildings in New York City and Washington, DC. Another hijacked plane crashed in a field in Shanksville, Pennsylvania. The 9/11 attacks killed nearly three thousand people and injured many more.

The terrorist attacks were the deadliest in modern times. People in North America feared future attacks. In the wake of 9/11, Canada passed the Anti-Terrorism Act in December 2001. This gave the government more authority to find and punish potential terrorists. And earlier that year, in October, the US had passed the Uniting and Strengthening America by Providing Appropriate Tools Required to Intercept and Obstruct Terrorism (USA PATRIOT) Act. This gave the US government broad power to surveil Americans through their use of communication technology, such as emails and voicemails, in the interest of identifying and catching terrorists. While many US citizens praised the act as enhancing national security, others worried that the act was violating citizens' civil liberties. According to the American Civil Liberties Union, a human rights organization, the act turned "regular citizens into suspects."

In 2000 Richard Butler, the leader of the Aryan Nations, led a small parade in Coeur d'Alene, Idaho. While some splinter groups of the Aryan Nations still exist, they have very few members.

CHAPTER SIX

Polarization and Suppression

Since the 1970s religious beliefs, demographics, and education as well as social ideologies including abortion, gun rights, and environmentalism had been further dividing US citizens. These divisions were also reflected in US political parties. Soon, the two major US parties shared few common beliefs or goals. Many people with strong political ideologies viewed members of the opposing party with increasing dislike and distrust. This polarization wasn't just apparent in the halls of the Capitol. More Democrats and Republicans claimed they would not want to live near, marry, or socialize with members of the opposing party. By the new millennium, US politics had become more polarized than ever before.

Bush vs. Gore

This division became even more evident in the close 2000 presidential election. Democrat Al Gore ran against Republican George W. Bush. More Americans voted for Gore than Bush, but that didn't mean Gore won the election. In the US, the popular vote does not decide the presidency;

the Electoral College does. Each state gets a certain number of electoral votes. Whichever candidate wins the most votes in a state gets that state's electoral votes.

Bush narrowly got more electoral votes than Gore. However, the election was too close to determine a winner. States began recounting their votes. The results of the election came down to Florida's twenty-five electoral votes. Whoever won Florida would win the election. Bush appeared to have only 327 more votes than Gore. It was close enough for the state to recount ballots manually. The candidates sued one another over the recounts.

Eventually, the dispute reached the Supreme Court. The court ruled in favor of Bush, awarding him Florida's electoral votes and granting him the presidency.

The 2000 election polarized Americans. Democrats felt the election had been stolen from them. Republicans accused Democrats of being sore losers. The election also showed how evenly the United States was divided between Democrats and Republicans. Parties sought new ways to increase their voter turnout while limiting the opposition's voters. For Republicans, that often meant rolling back voter rights to restrict the opposition's turnout. For Democrats, that meant attracting new voters to their party and getting them to the polls.

Voter Suppression

Since the 1990s the Republican Party has aimed to reduce the number of Democratic voters. Just before the 2000 election, Florida Republicans hired a private company to purge voter rolls. This meant deleting voters who were no longer eligible. However, the company deleted many voters who were still eligible. These voters were disproportionately Black Democrats. In one county, 65 percent of the eligible voters deleted were Black, even though Black people made up just over 20 percent of the population there.

After the 2000 election, many Republican-led states and counties enacted laws making it harder to vote, especially in Democratic-leaning areas. These included laws requiring voters to show identification to vote. Such laws disproportionately affected young people and urban residents, who were less likely to have a driver's license as their primary ID. In some states, Republican officials limited voting hours and closed polling places early in Democrat-leaning counties. State legislatures also practiced gerrymandering.

Voter Identification Laws in Effect

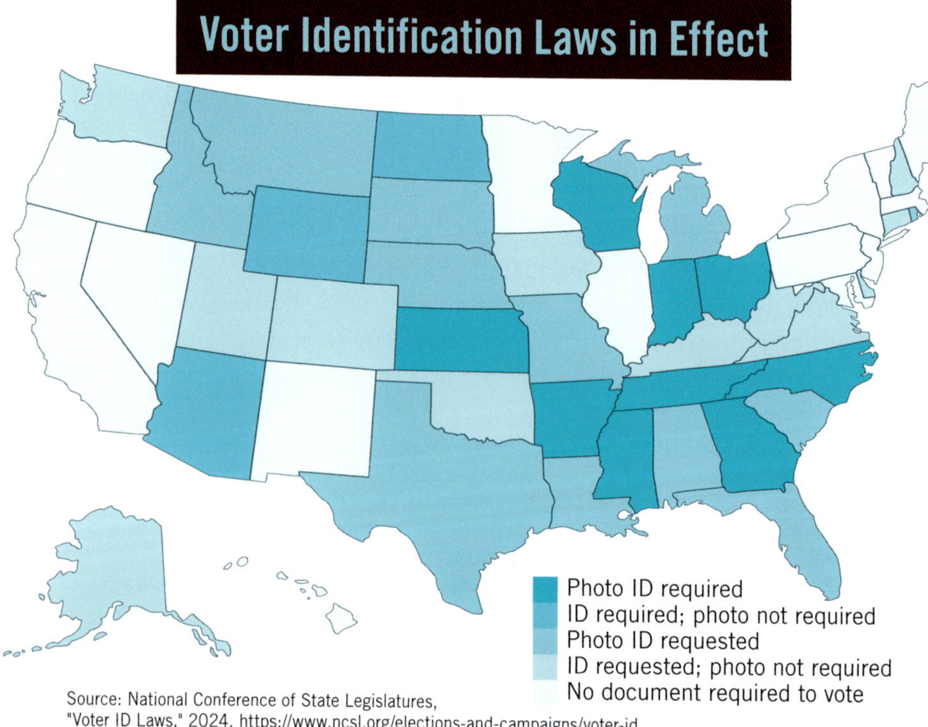

Source: National Conference of State Legislatures, "Voter ID Laws," 2024, https://www.ncsl.org/elections-and-campaigns/voter-id.

As of 2024, thirty-six states have laws requiring or asking voters to show some form of identification. The other fourteen states and Washington, DC, have alternate ways to verify the identities of voters.

This involved redrawing voting district maps so there were more Republican-leaning districts and fewer Democrat-leaning ones. Many states also passed laws banning felons from voting, even after they'd completed their sentences. This law disproportionately affected Black and non-white Hispanic people, who are far more likely to be imprisoned than white people. These groups statistically are more likely to vote Democrat. Other laws affected other Democrat-skewing voting groups, such as Indigenous Americans. Indigenous people are much less likely to have the documentation such as birth certificates required for state IDs, which they must have to register to vote in many states. In 2018 a North Dakota law banned using PO boxes as addresses for voter registration. This disproportionately affected Indigenous people living on reservations, who often relied on PO boxes due to a lack of named streets.

REFLECT

What are some of the advantages and disadvantages of electing presidents based on the electoral vote rather than the popular vote?

Fighting Fraud?

While Democrats argue that Republicans are suppressing voting rights to win elections, Republicans claim to be fighting voter fraud, or illegal interference in an election by voters. This can include voting more than once, voting under a false name, or pressuring voters to vote for a certain candidate. Voter fraud has been a frequently discussed issue, particularly among Republicans, since the 1990s. But the 2000 presidential election brought voter fraud to the public's attention. Republicans passed laws that made voting more difficult in the name of protecting election integrity.

However, despite the amount of attention the issue received, many studies showed that voter fraud was nonexistent.

Despite the lack of evidence, many Republicans continued to sound the alarm on voter fraud. In 2008 US voters elected the country's first Black president, Barack Obama. Many Republicans said the election had been rigged, particularly in primarily Black areas of cities such as Chicago and Philadelphia. Following Obama's inauguration, sixteen states passed new voter ID requirements. Still, Obama won reelection in 2012. Although the voter fraud claims didn't change the election results, they undermined the public's confidence in free and fair elections.

Voter Fraud Then and Now

Experts, analysts, and election officials alike have found voter fraud to be rare in modern US elections. But this wasn't always the case. In the 1800s and early 1900s voter fraud was rampant. Organizations called political machines often controlled local elections. They used bribery and other methods to make sure their preferred candidates got elected. In the mid-1800s a Democratic political machine in New York City arranged citizenship for new immigrants in exchange for votes. They encouraged voters to cast multiple ballots by using fake names and shaving off their beards between votes. They threatened voters who resisted with physical violence. Political machines found ways to cheat at elections in other areas, including stuffing ballot boxes and changing ballots that had already been cast. Over the next century, new technology and laws, including secret ballots and harsh punishments for cheating, helped reduce voter fraud.

CHAPTER SEVEN

Democracy in Peril

With Obama's election, Black Americans finally had a leader in the nation's highest office who looked like them. However, like many Black Americans, Obama faced daily racism and prejudice. He was the target of racist attacks throughout his presidency. One of the most prominent was a conspiracy theory about his birthplace.

Spreading Lies

During Obama's 2008 campaign, right-wing activists spread false rumors that his birth certificate was fake and that he had been born in Kenya, not Hawaii. Obama released multiple versions of his birth certificate, but the rumors persisted throughout his presidency. Celebrity businessman Donald Trump became one of the biggest supporters of the so-called birther conspiracy. The birther conspiracy highlighted a new issue facing global democracy—misinformation. As Internet use spread and social media became more prominent, misinformation reshaped US politics for years to come.

In 2016 Trump became the Republican presidential nominee. He used misinformation as a tool throughout

After being elected in 2016, Trump kept about 44 percent of the promises he made during his campaign.

his campaign. While politicians are often known for exaggerating facts to support their message, Trump took this tactic further. He spread outright lies about his personal finances; the economy; his Democratic opponent, Hillary Clinton; and even suggested that a rival Republican's father was involved in assassinating a US president. The election was close. In the end, Clinton won the popular vote, but Trump won the electoral vote. He was inaugurated on January 20, 2017.

Trump's 2016 Presidency

Trump was very different from previous US presidents. He was a celebrity businessman with little political experience. Trump embraced both Populist and Nationalist ideas that leaned much farther right than previous presidents. Trump promised to reduce immigration and renegotiate agreements with US allies to benefit the US. He argued for a strong executive branch, openly admiring authoritarian leaders such as Russia's Vladimir Putin. He also used dog whistles, or subtle messaging, to support racist and sexist ideas that appealed to white supremacist groups around the country. For example, in 2017 white supremacist groups held a political rally called Unite the Right in Charlottesville, Virginia. The protesters marched through the city's streets, saying racist slurs and declaring their support for Trump. The rally turned deadly when a protester drove a car into a crowd of counter-protesters. Rather than condemning the racist attacks, Trump declared there were "very fine people on both sides." Many viewed this as a subtle showing of support for white supremacist ideas.

Right-Wing Extremism around the World

Trump's rise to power was part of a wave of right-wing extremism that was taking place around the world. Right-wing terrorists in typically peaceful countries, including New Zealand and Norway, had launched deadly attacks throughout the 2010s. Populist politicians were also rising to power across Europe and South America. In Canada, smaller, isolated extremist groups began organizing into larger coalitions. These groups became especially active online, spreading their ideas through social media, memes, and websites. In 2018 Canada's government launched a new initiative to fight the spread of extremism online. In 2021 the Canadian government also declared the US right-wing extremist group the Proud Boys a terrorist organization.

The 2020 Election

In 2020 Trump ran for reelection against Democratic candidate Joe Biden. The election took place during the global COVID-19 pandemic. As a result, many voters cast ballots by mail rather than at the polls. Because of the number of mail-in ballots, it took weeks to count the results. In the end, Biden won both the popular and electoral votes. He was declared the winner. However, Trump refused to accept the election results.

Trump claimed, without evidence, that Biden had stolen the election. He began doing everything in his power to overturn the results. He personally called election officials in several swing states, including Georgia, Arizona, and Michigan. He asked them to replace Biden's electors with electors who would vote for him when the Electoral College met in December. Trump asked Georgia's secretary of state to "find 11,780 votes," the number he would need to win the state. He demanded that Justice Department officials open investigations into cases of voter fraud despite lack of evidence. He pressured his vice president, Mike Pence, to decertify the election results. All state and federal officials refused to aid Trump in overturning the election, and on January 6, 2021, US Congress met to certify the election results.

"I voted for you. I worked for you. I campaigned for you. I just won't do anything illegal for you."

—Arizona congressman Rusty Bowers

January 6 Insurrection

While Congress met, Trump held a rally with his supporters nearby. During the rally, he gave a speech denying the election results and urging his supporters to fight back. He

Decoding QAnon

Conspiracy theories became a major part of US democracy during Trump's presidency. These ideas circulated the Internet, gaining traction. One of the most prominent sources was an anonymous poster called QAnon, or Q for short. Q's first posts appeared in 2016 on a web forum called 4chan. The posts were coded messages claiming that a group of devil worshippers secretly ran the Democratic Party. According to Q, Trump was the only person who could stop the Democrats' evil agenda. The posts gained supporters, and by 2020 more than 17 percent of US citizens believed Q's claims. QAnon's supporters included prominent Republican lawmakers. The account posted false information about the COVID-19 pandemic and the Black Lives Matter protests. QAnon also made vague predictions about future actions Trump would take. After Trump's loss in 2020, QAnon supported his claims that the election had been stolen. Q's followers flooded the Internet with more theories and ideas. Experts have since determined that QAnon was most likely a software engineer from South Africa.

encouraged them to march to the Capitol to show their dissent. Following Trump's speech, a mob of more than one thousand armed Trump supporters, including members of the Proud Boys and other right-wing extremist groups, stormed the US Capitol. They forced their way past the police and into the building. Some threatened to find and kill Pence and Democratic leaders.

The extremists vandalized the Capitol. Some lawmakers were evacuated, stopping the election certification. Others

The Capitol rioters caused about $2.8 million of damage to the Capitol. In the year following the attack, the Federal Bureau of Investigation and the Justice Department arrested more than one thousand rioters.

barricaded themselves in offices and closets. Law enforcement cleared the extremists from the Capitol after about four hours. Seven people died during the insurrection, and hundreds of others were injured, including more than 150 police officers. Early the next morning, Congress reconvened to finish certifying the results. Lawmakers voted to impeach Trump over his role in inciting the riot, but he was later acquitted.

Misinformation

Many experts believed the January 6 insurrection resulted from misinformation, which had been spreading online.

Shortly after his 2016 election, Trump used the term "fake news" to describe media coverage that portrayed him negatively. He especially targeted left-leaning news organizations, such as the *New York Times* and CNN. Meanwhile, he praised right-leaning news organizations that ran flattering stories about him, such as Breitbart and Fox News. Other politicians also adopted this tactic.

Many people shifted toward news sources supporting their political views. In 2020, 65 percent of Republicans trusted Fox News as their primary news media source. Similarly, 67 percent of Democrats trusted CNN as their primary news source. However, many Democrats found several other news sources to be trustworthy too. Republicans overwhelmingly preferred Fox News. This polarization meant Americans were getting their news from radically different sources covering stories from very different perspectives.

Meanwhile, more people were getting news from social media sources, such as X, Facebook, and TikTok. Unlike the news media, these sources often contained false information. Memes and articles sharing conspiracy theories and fake stories circulated widely. Much of this was propaganda with an agenda. During the 2020 election, Russian-based groups known as troll farms reached more than 140 million Americans per month on Facebook. They spread false information that was damaging to Biden and flattering to Trump. Many US officials believed the Russian government had coordinated the spread of misinformation to improve Trump's chances of winning.

REFLECT

What are some possible solutions to the issue of political polarization in the US and around the world?

CHAPTER EIGHT

The Future of Democracy

Trump's first presidency (2016–2020) was a turbulent time in US and global politics. But despite the unrest and Trump and his allies' attempts to overturn the election, the democratic process prevailed. On January 20, 2021, Joe Biden became the forty-sixth US president. While most Republicans disagreed with Biden, many Americans hoped for a more peaceful political period. Despite some Republican claims of a stolen 2020 election, most lawmakers accepted its fairness.

Still, most experts believed Trump was not the cause but a symptom of a decades-long shift in right-wing ideology toward extremism. In 2024 Trump won the presidential election for the second time. While some people celebrated this win, others wondered what it might mean for the democratic process in the future.

Preserving Democracy

In 1958, 73 percent of Americans claimed they could trust the federal government. But by the 2020s public trust in the US government was at its lowest point. In 2024 only 22 percent of Americans said they trusted the government to do the right thing most of the time. But many people and organizations make it their mission to preserve democracy and ensure the US government works for everyone.

Nonprofit organizations such as the Anti-Defamation League and the Southern Poverty Law Center have been working to fight extremism for decades. They monitor and analyze extremist activity and incidents of hate speech. The US government also works to prevent potential extremists from becoming radicalized in the first place. In 2021 Biden announced the first ever strategy to combat US domestic terrorism. The National Strategy for Countering Domestic Terrorism included preventing recruitment and confronting existing terrorist groups.

Analyzing Extremism

In 2022 a group of researchers released an in-depth study comparing three kinds of political extremism. The paper was the first of its kind and focused on the differences between Islamic, right-wing, and left-wing extremism. The researchers looked at examples of extremism in the US and around the world. The studies found that both right- and left-wing extremists had many traits in common. Both used strong, angry language to convey their beliefs. They also showed low tolerance for differing viewpoints. However, right-wing and Islamic extremists were far more likely to act on their beliefs through violent acts. The study found that left-wing extremists were 68 percent less likely to engage in violence on behalf of their beliefs.

Battling Misinformation

Other nonprofits and lawmakers have taken steps to combat the spread of misinformation online. The Polarization and Extremism Research and Innovation Lab and the Southern Poverty Law Center's Learning for Justice program train people on how to detect propaganda and misinformation. They encourage teachers and guardians to teach young people how to fact-check claims and come to their own conclusions. The Learning for Justice program encourages people to ask a series of questions when analyzing a piece of content. These include:

- What is the source, and do they have a specific agenda, perspective, or purpose?
- Can the information be verified through other reliable and non-biased sources?
- What is the content's purpose? Is it designed to persuade or inform the reader? Is there any bias in the content?
- Why and how was the content created? What perspectives are included? What perspectives are missing?

Social media has been one of the primary means of spreading misinformation. In 2016 Facebook began partnering with fact-checking companies to verify posts. Users who try to share misinformation see a warning that the information is false. In 2023 X added a feature where users can fact-check posts. But social media companies are secretive about their inner workings. Facebook won't share what percentage of posts are fact-checked. And social media remains a key method for distributing misinformation and radicalizing extremists. However, organizations are also working to combat hate and misinformation on social media. The Center for Countering Digital Hate (CCDH) works to stop the spread of hateful content and misinformation on social media sites through research, marketing campaigns, and policy changes.

Other organizations fighting misinformation include FactCheck.org, the News Literacy Project, and the Institute for Strategic Dialogue. FactCheck.org counters misinformation and deception in US politics by fact-checking statements made by US politicians in TV ads, interviews, and debates. The News Literacy Project, an educational nonprofit, helps people assess media credibility. It offers educators tools to teach students and provides free resources such as podcasts, apps, quizzes, and more to identify media bias and misinformation. The Institute for Strategic Dialogue focuses on reducing political polarization, extremism, and misinformation online. It conducts thorough research and uses its findings to propose policy changes.

Imran Ahmed is the CEO of CCDH. CCDH's research has revealed how digital platforms not only promote but also profit from hate and extremism. CCDH has found consistent failures by social media companies to act on harmful content, which can feed political extremism and erode democracy.

Protecting Voters

Other groups aim to make sure every voice is heard. Voting rights groups push for laws safeguarding voting rights. They also assist with voter registration and encouraging voter turnout. After losing the Georgia gubernatorial election in 2018, Stacey Abrams founded the nonprofit Fair Fight to advocate for voter rights. The organization focuses on helping disenfranchised voters, including young people and voters of color.

> "Voting is not magic. Democracy is not magic, but it is the medicine we needed to start to treat the challenges and the ills of our society."
>
> —Stacey Abrams

Studies have shown that white people are far more likely to vote than Black people, non-white Hispanic people, or Asian Americans. Experts believe this is related to the long history of racial bias, discrimination, and voter suppression people of color have faced. Fair Fight inspired more than eight hundred thousand new voters to register in 2020. It is widely credited with boosting Georgia's voter turnout to its highest in history during the 2020 election. Many of these voters supported Democrats, helping turn the usually Republican state into a win for Democrats.

The voter turnout for the 2020 election was historically high across the rest of the country too. More than two-thirds of eligible voters cast ballots. The wide availability of mail-in ballots and early voting made it easier for older adults and those with disabilities to cast their votes. Nearly half of all voters cast ballots by mail that year. While activism can drive change, voting remains one of the most powerful ways for citizens in a democracy to make their voices heard.

Other organizations are dedicated to encouraging young people to vote. People between the ages of eighteen and

In 2011 activists in New York City protested against stricter voting laws. They argued that requiring photo IDs, reducing early voting days, and making it harder to register would prevent many people from being able to vote.

twenty-nine often face barriers to voting, especially in states with strict voting laws. Young voters are less likely to have a permanent address, state ID, easy access to polling sites, or an understanding of how the voter registration process works. Rock the Vote was established in 1990 to help register young voters. It allows voters to check their registration status online and find their nearest polling place. NextGen America is another voting organization that connects with youth, often using technology. Since 2013 the organization has registered more than 1.5 million young people to vote.

REFLECT

What do you think is the best tool for protecting democracy and fighting extremism? Why?

CONCLUSION

Building the Future

Democracy has changed much from the early days of ancient Athens and the Iroquois Confederacy. Modern governments have many more citizens with diverse backgrounds, wants, and needs. Still, democracy remains a powerful tool for turning the voices of many into a functioning government. Important social changes from the Nineteenth Amendment to the civil rights movement are the result of groups of people coming together to make their voices heard.

Throughout history, North American nations have faced great threats to their democracies, from voter suppression to political extremism. However, these nations have risen to the challenge, taking steps to preserve the democratic principles their countries were founded on, including liberty, equality, and the right of citizens to actively participate in their government. There is still more work to be done to make sure democracy is fair for everyone. The hard work of voters, activists, organizations, and leaders gives hope for a brighter future. With continued effort and dedication, we can build a future where everyone's voice is heard, political extremism is kept in check, and democracy works for all people equally.

Help Build the Future

You can help support democracy and fight extremism too. Here are some ways you can do so on your own or in your community:

- **Stay informed.** Regularly follow credible news sources and stay updated on current events.
- **Practice media literacy.** Be critical with any piece of content you view or read. Consider what its source is, why the piece was created, whether it shows bias, and whether the information can be fact-checked in another credible source.
- **Volunteer.** Look for ways to support the causes you care about. You could offer to register voters, volunteer for political campaigns, or support a nonprofit that shares your beliefs.
- **Share sparingly.** Practice media literacy with every piece of content you view on social media. If it doesn't meet all the criteria, don't share it.
- **Participate in the process.** Be an active member of your local government. Attend city council or school board meetings. Contact your representatives by email, phone, or mail to discuss issues you care about.
- **Make your voice heard.** If you're eligible to vote, cast your ballot on Election Day. If you're not eligible, make sure you're up-to-date on the current issues and candidates. Know how to register and where your local polling place is. Encourage older family members, community members, and friends to vote.
- **Foster inclusive communities.** Help promote understanding and inclusivity among different groups in your community. Challenge existing biases or prejudices you observe. Pay attention to any unintentional biases you might hold. Actively oppose discrimination based on race, religion, gender, or other identities.

GLOSSARY

abolitionist: a person who works to end enslavement and fights for the freedom of all enslaved people

acquit: to find someone not guilty of a criminal charge

authoritarian: relating to a form of government in which a leader demands absolute obedience from the subjects and which features a strong central government

autocracy: a form of government in which a single ruler has the power to make all decisions

boycott: an organized refusal to interact with a product or group for political reasons

bribe: an illegal gift, favor, or money given to influence a decision or action

Communism: an economic and political system in which property, businesses, and goods are owned and controlled by the government and are available to people as needed

constitution: a set of rules or guidelines that dictate how a government functions

demographics: statistical data that describes the characteristics of a population such as age, gender, income, education level, and ethnicity. This data is used to understand who makes up a population and how they are different from each other.

disenfranchise: to deprive of legal rights, such as the right to vote

dissent: to disagree with

draft: a process in which citizens are selected for mandatory military service

Fascism: an ideology that emphasizes a single powerful leader and the needs of the nation over individual rights, often restricting individual liberties

felon: a person who has been convicted of committing a felony, such as robbery, assault, or use of illegal substances

gerrymandering: the practice of dividing a region into election districts in a way that gives an unfair advantage to one political party

ideology: a collection of ideas or beliefs; a way of thinking of an individual or a group

impeach: to formally accuse a high-ranking official, such as the president, of wrongdoing or misconduct, often leading to a trial to decide whether they should be removed from office

inaugurate: to induct a public official into political office

insurrection: an act of rebellion against a government

militia: a group of people organized for military purposes but who are not in the armed forces

Nationalist: relating to Nationalism, the strong attachment to and loyalty toward one's own country and culture that often is at the expense of other countries and cultures

parliament: a legislative body of government, typically found in democratic countries, in which elected representatives gather to make and pass laws. Canada, Great Britain, and other countries have parliaments.

Populist: relating to a belief in the power of regular people to control their government, rather than a small group of powerful elites

propaganda: information intended to make people feel or think a certain way

radical: holding views on an issue that are more extreme than those of most people. To radicalize is to persuade a person to share a set of extreme views.

ratify: to pass into law

recession: a prolonged decrease in economic growth

segregate: to forcibly separate individuals or groups based on certain characteristics such as race, ethnicity, religion, or gender

sit-in: an act of protest in which a person or group of people enters a space and refuses to leave until certain demands are met

Socialist: relating to Socialism, an economic system in which wealth and resources are shared equally

suffrage: the right to vote

swing state: a US state in which Democrats and Republicans are relatively evenly divided, giving that state disproportional influence in a national election

veto: the power of one government official or branch to stop an action by another official or branch

SOURCE NOTES

14 "No mobs, no confusion, no tumult.": Stacy Schiff, "The Boston Tea Party Was More Than That. It Was a Riot," *New York Times*, August 13, 2020, https://www.nytimes.com/2020/08/13/opinion/protests-monuments-history.html.

16 "A Constitution, which . . . immediate aristocratic tyrant.": Mercy Otis Warren, "Observations on the New Constitution (1788)," National Constitution Center, accessed May 10, 2024, https://constitutioncenter.org/the-constitution/historic-document-library/detail/mercy-otis-warren-observations-on-the-new-constitution-1788.

21 "All persons born . . . the United States.": Brandon Tensley, "America's Long History of Black Voter Suppression," CNN Politics, accessed May 9, 2024, https://www.cnn.com/interactive/2021/05/politics/black-voting-rights-suppression-timeline/.

22 "The right of . . . condition of servitude.": "15th Amendment to the US Constitution: Voting Rights (1870)," National Archives, accessed May 9, 2024, https://www.archives.gov/milestone-documents/15th-amendment#transcript.

26 "A man's rights . . . of her sex.": "Frederick Douglass (1818–1895)," Oregon Secretary of State LaVonne Griffin-Valade, accessed May 9, 2024, https://sos.oregon.gov/archives/exhibits/suffrage/Pages/bio/douglass.aspx.

28 "Do you know . . . my own government.": Mr. Trout, Mr. Trout, Georgia, Manuscript/Mixed Material, accessed May 9, 2024, https://www.loc.gov/item/wpalh000540/.

35 "regular citizens into suspects.": "Surveillance Under the Patriot Act," American Civil Liberties Union, accessed August 15, 2024, https://www.aclu.org/issues/national-security/privacy-and-surveillance/surveillance-under-patriot-act.

43 "very fine people on both sides.": Debbie Elliott, "The Charlottesville Rally 5 Years Later: 'It's What You're Still Trying to Forget,'" NPR, August 12, 2022, https://www.npr.org/2022/08/12/1116942725/the-charlottesville-rally-5-years-later-its-what-youre-still-trying-to-forget.

44 "I voted for . . . illegal for you.": Laura Romero, "'The Signing': What to Know about the Arizona Attorney General's 2020 Election

Probe," ABC News, April 5, 2024, https://abcnews.go.com/US/signing-arizona-attorney-generals-2020-election-probe/story?id=108864060.

44 "find 11,780 votes": Rachel Treisman, "'Georgia Officials Fact-Check an Infamous Trump Phone Call in Real Time," MPR News, June 21, 2022, https://www.npr.org/2022/06/21/1106472863/georgia-officials-fact-check-infamous-trump-phone-call-in-real time.

52 "Voting is not . . . of our society.": Jonathan Heeter, "Stacey Abrams Continues to Fight for Voter Rights," American University Washington, DC, February 24, 2024, https://www.american.edu/news/stacey-abrams-kpu-voting.cfm.

SELECTED BIBLIOGRAPHY

"About Parties and Leadership | Historical Overview." United States Senate. Accessed May 9, 2024. https://www.senate.gov/about/origins-foundations/parties-leadership/overview.htm.

"Block the Vote: How Politicians are Trying to Block Voters from the Ballot Box." ACLU. Last updated August 18, 2021. https://www.aclu.org/news/civil-liberties/block-the-vote-voter-suppression-in-2020.

Britton-Purdy, Jedediah. "We've Been Thinking About America's Trust Collapse All Wrong." *Atlantic*, January 8, 2024. https://www.theatlantic.com/ideas/archive/2024/01/trust-democracy-liberal-government/677035/.

Jasko, Katarzyna, et al. "A Comparison of Political Violence by Left-Wing, Right-Wing, and Islamist Extremists in the United States and the World." *Proceedings of the National Academy of Sciences of the United States of America*, vol. 119 (30), 2022. https://www.ncbi.nlm.nih.gov/pmc/articles/PMC9335287/.

Keane, John. *The Shortest History of Democracy: 4,000 Years of Self-Government—A Retelling for Our Times*. New York: The Experiment, 2022.

Moore, Derick. "July 4th: Celebrating 243 Years of Independence." United States Census Bureau, July 2, 2019. https://www.census.gov/library/stories/2019/07/july-fourth-celebrating-243-years-of-independence.html.

FURTHER INFORMATION

Books

Fleischer, Jeff. *Votes of Confidence: A Young Person's Guide to American Elections*. Minneapolis: Zest Books, 2024.
Read all about US elections in the third edition of this guide. Targeted especially toward new and future voters, it contains up-to-date statistics and explanations with current and historic examples.

Harris, Duchess. *Politics and Civil Unrest in Modern America*. Minneapolis: Core Library, 2021.
This book explores the ways in which the US government responds to civic unrest and activism. Learn about some of the ways lawmakers are working to prevent police violence and keep protests safe for everyone.

Miller-Idriss, Cynthia. *Hate in the Homeland: The New Global Far Right*. Princeton, New Jersey: Princeton University Press, 2022.
Learn about topics related to extremism, including hate crimes, misinformation, and conspiracy theories, while exploring the ways far-right extremists recruit young people to their cause.

Rockler, Naomi. *The Facts about Election and Voter Fraud*. San Diego: Reference Point, 2024.
Explore the facts and fiction surrounding the issue of election fraud. Learn about ballot miscounting, voting machines, and how uncommon voter fraud really is.

Tyner, Artika R. *Black Achievements in Politics: Celebrating Shirley Chisholm, Barack Obama, and More*. Minneapolis: Lerner Publications, 2024.
Learn about some of the achievements Black politicians have made and some of the ways they have worked to improve their communities.

Websites

Americans Are Tired of Political Division. Here's How to Bridge It

https://time.com/6266873/american-political-division-courage-challenge/

This article interviews two experts about the history of political polarization, current views on it, and how the issue can be solved.

Black Voter Suppression

https://www.cnn.com/interactive/2021/05/politics/black-voting-rights-suppression-timeline/

This interactive timeline explores the long history of Black voter suppression in the US.

Freedom House: Countries and Territories

https://freedomhouse.org/countries/nations-transit/scores

This website provides global freedom scores measuring democracy in countries around the world.

Political Parties

https://www.loc.gov/classroom-materials/elections/presidential-election-process/political-parties/

Learn all about US political parties at this website from the US Library of Congress.

Preserving Democracy

https://www.pbs.org/wnet/preserving-democracy/

Visit this website to learn how different US state leaders are working to preserve democracy.

INDEX

abolitionist, 19–21, 26
Abrams, Stacey, 52
activists, 6, 25, 27–34, 41, 52–54
  anti–Vietnam War, 29–32
  civil rights, 27–29
  left-wing, 32–33
  right-wing, 41
Age of Enlightenment, 9–10, 12
Amendment, 21–22, 26, 54
  Fifteenth, 22
  Fourteenth, 21
  Nineteenth, 26, 54
American Civil Liberties Union, 35
Anti-Defamation League, 49
Anti-Terrorism Act, 35
authoritarian governments, 14, 24, 43

ballots, 22, 26, 37, 40, 44, 52
Biden, Joe, 44, 47–49
Black Lives Matter, 31, 45
Bloody Sunday, 27
boycotts, 28
British colonies, 12–14, 18
Bush, George W., 36–37

Capitol, US, 36, 44–46
Center for Countering Digital Hate (CCDH), 51
Chicano Moratorium, 30–32
civil rights movement, 27–29, 54
civil war, 10–11, 20–21
  English, 10–11
  US, 20–21
Clinton, Hillary, 42
Communism, 29, 32
Constitution, 10–11, 14–16, 21–22, 25
  British, 11, 25
  Canadian, 25
  US, 10, 14–16, 21–22

ecoterrorism, 32–34
elections, 4, 6, 9, 14, 18–19, 21–23, 25, 36–42, 44–48, 52, 55
  certification of, 44–46
  gubernatorial, 52
  presidential, 18–19, 21, 23, 36–42, 44–48
Electoral College, 36–38
electoral votes, 37, 39, 42, 44
enslavement, 5, 18–22
extremism, 6, 13, 19, 28, 31–35, 43, 45–46, 48–51, 53–55
  Islamic, 34–35, 49
  left-wing, 32–34, 49
  religious, 34–35
  right-wing, 43, 45–46, 48–49

FactCheck.org, 51
Fair Fight, 52
feudalism, 8–9
founding fathers, 14–15
French Revolution, 17

Gore, Al, 36–37
Greece, 4–5, 7, 54

Institute for Strategic Dialogue, 51
Iroquois Confederacy, 7–8, 54

Jackson, Andrew, 18–19
Jackson, Jimmie Lee, 27
January 6 insurrection, 44–46

King, Martin Luther, Jr., 27

Locke, John, 10

Magna Carta, 11
media, 6, 18, 41, 43, 47, 50–51, 55
  literacy, 55
  news, 47, 51, 55
  social, 41, 43, 47, 50–51, 55
Mexico, 6, 8, 12, 23–24
  ancient democracies in, 8
  colonization in, 12
misinformation, 6, 41–42, 46–47, 50–51

National Strategy for Countering
Domestic Terrorism, 49
News Literacy Project, 51
NextGen America, 53

Obama, Barack, 40–41

Pence, Mike, 44–45
political parties, 10, 16–22, 26, 36–40, 44–45, 47–48, 52
  Democratic, 19, 21–22, 26, 28, 36–40, 42, 44–45, 47–48, 52
  Democratic-Republicans, 16, 18–19
  Federalist, 16, 18
  Republican, 19–21, 28, 36–42, 45, 47–48, 52
  Whig, 19
political polarization, 6, 36–37, 47, 50–51
popular vote, 36, 39, 42, 44
protests, 13–14, 23, 27–32, 43, 45, 53
  anti–Vietnam War, 29–32
  Black Lives Matter, 31, 45
  civil rights, 27–29
  colonial, 13–14
  in Mexico, 23
  liberal, 32
  voting law, 27, 53
  white supremacist, 43
Proud Boys, 43, 45

QAnon, 45

Rankin, Jeannette, 25–26
Revels, Hiram, 21
Rock the Vote, 53
Rousseau, Jean-Jacques, 10

San Diego, Daniel Andreas, 33–34
sit-ins, 28, 33
slavery, *See* enslavement
Snyder Act, 26
Southern Poverty Law Center, 49–50
Students for a Democratic Society (SDS), 29, 32
Symbionese Liberation Army (SLA), 32–33

terrorism, 21, 33–35, 43, 49
Trump, Donald, 41–48
Turner, Nat, 20

Vietnam War, 29–32, *See also* protests: anti–Vietnam War
voter fraud, 39–40, 44
voter registration, 27, 38–39, 52–53, 55
voter suppression, 6, 21–22, 37–39, 52–53
voting rights, 6, 15, 21–22, 25–28, 37–39, 52–53
  groups, 52
  of Black people, 6, 15, 21–22, 26–28, 37–39
  of felons, 39
  of Indigenous people, 6, 15, 25–26, 39
  of women, 6, 15, 25–26
Voting Rights Act, 27–28

Weather Underground, 32
white supremacists, 21, 24, 28, 31, 34–35, 43
World War II, 24, 26, 29

ABOUT THE AUTHOR

Elsie Olson is a writer from Minnetrista, Minnesota. She has written many fiction and nonfiction books for young readers. Her areas of expertise include science and history. When not writing, she enjoys gardening, trail running, cross-country skiing, and spending time with her family.

PHOTO ACKNOWLEDGMENTS

The images in this book are used with the permission of: © Wikimedia Commons, pp. 5, 17, 30; © New York (State). Commission, Jamestown Exposition, 1907/Flickr, p. 8; © Godfrey Kneller/Wikimedia Commons, p. 10; © David Smart/Shutterstock Images, p. 11; © IanDagnall Computing/Alamy Photo, p. 12; © Howard Chandler Christy/Wikimedia Commons, p. 15; © AOC Photo Branch/Flickr, p. 16; © Library of Congress; P&P/, p. 19; © Brady-Handy photograph collection/ Wikimedia Commons, p. 21; © Adam Cuerden/Wikimedia Commons, p. 26; © Alpha Historica/Alamy Photo, p. 27; © Dan Aasland/Wikimedia Commons, p. 31; © John Malmin, Los Angeles Times/Wikimedia Commons, p. 33; © TOM DAVENPORT/AP Images, p. 35; © Giraphics/ Shutterstock Images, p. 38; © The White House/Wikimedia Commons, p. 42; © TapTheForwardAssist/Wikimedia Commons, p. 46; © Mark Thomas/Alamy Photo, p. 51; © Richard Levine/Alamy Photo, p. 53.

Cover Photo: © Derek Hatfield/Shutterstock Images

Design Elements: © Ezhevika/Shutterstock Images